To my dear student
Brian Zuleta with
sincere best wishes,

Celestino Heeres

THE RELUCTANT REVOLUTIONARY

Printed in Victoria, Canada

National Library of Canada Cataloguing in Publication Data

Heres, Celestino, 1935-
        The reluctant revolutionary / Celestino Heres.
ISBN 1-55395-606-0
        I. Title.
F1787.5.H47 2003   972.9106'3'092   C2003-900233-0

TRAFFORD

This book was published *on-demand* in cooperation with Trafford Publishing.
On-demand publishing is a unique process and service of making a book available
for retail sale to the public taking advantage of on-demand manufacturing and
Internet marketing. **On-demand publishing** includes promotions, retail sales,
manufacturing, order fulfilment, accounting and collecting royalties on behalf of
the author.

Suite 6E, 2333 Government St., Victoria, B.C. V8T 4P4, CANADA

Phone	250-383-6864	Toll-free	1-888-232-4444 (Canada & US)
Fax	250-383-6804	E-mail	sales@trafford.com
Web site	www.trafford.com	TRAFFORD PUBLISHING IS A DIVISION OF TRAFFORD

HOLDINGS LTD.

Trafford Catalogue #02-1322   www.trafford.com/robots/02-1322.html

10   9   8   7   6   5   4   3   2

CONTENTS

PHOTOGRAPHS

PREFACE

This book is not intended as a biography but rather a recounting of a chapter in my personal history that took me from my beloved homeland to an exiled life in the United States. It is intended as a recollection of important life experiences that drove me to be a reluctant revolutionary.

This book had to be written because it contains the knowledge of a witness who was very close to historical events whose details are not readily available from any other source. The names of all the characters are real. It also had to be written in English so that non-Spanish speaking people can learn the truth about what really happened in Cuba during the ousting of Fulgencio Batista and the impact of communism on the island. The author's expectation is that this work will offer a perspective that will make readers more appreciative of the suffering of the Cuban people. This suffering was caused by the betrayal of the leaders of the Cuban revolution and by the influence of the United States government in Cuban affairs.

Celestino Heres, Ph.D., is a retired professor of Computer Systems at the University of Connecticut at Stamford and at the Norwalk Community Technical College, Norwalk, Conn. He is now teaching at Brien McMahon High School in Norwalk. Born and raised in Cuba, Dr. Heres graduated from North Carolina State University in Raleigh, N.C. He has been an educator and Computer Systems consultant to Perkin-Elmer, Dun & Bradstreet, and many other corporations. His wife, Elsa, is a bilingual teacher at Silvermine Elementary School in Norwalk. Their two daughters, Elsa Marie, an elementary school teacher, and Arleen, a U.S. Postal Inspector share the same dream of their parents: to

someday visit their beloved Cuba, a free Cuba.

Dr. Heres and his wife reside in Norwalk.

Dedication

I dedicate this book to my partner in life, Elsa, my wife. Without her devoted love and encouragement I would not have been able to relive some very painful experiences and, as a result, be able to write them down. I also wish to dedicate this book to the Cuban people all over the world, both living and deceased, who have not been able to return to their motherland for political reasons.

Acknowledgement

My thanks to my friends Jorge Martinez Jr., grandson of one of the characters in the book, for his excellent suggestions and to Richard Anderson for his brilliant editing of my notes. Also to both my daughter Elsa Marie and my son-in-law John Hungaski Jr., for designing the front cover of the book.

Yo quiero cuando yo muera

sin Patria pero sin amo,

tener en mi tumba un ramo

de flores y una bandera.

José Marti, Poeta cubano

When I die, without a country

but without a master,

I wish to have in my grave

a bouquet of flowers and a flag.

José Marti, Cuban poet

Chapter One: My Return to Cuba

It was late in the summer of 1958, and, after completing three and a half years of engineering studies at North Carolina State University, I decided to return to Cuba to visit my family that I had not seen since I started my studies. One of the reasons I went to North Carolina in the United States was I wanted to major in Mechanical Engineering, and, at that time, there was no such major at the University of Havana. Also, there had been political demonstrations and protests at the University of Havana, and I was afraid I might not be able to complete my studies there.

My home was in a small town named after Christopher Columbus, which, in Spanish, is Colón, and was not too far from the Bay of Pigs and the mountains of south Cuba called

El Escambray. I knew that the situation in Cuba was dangerous because of the revolution against the dictator Fulgencio Batista. I had no fear for my personal safety because my family had never been involved in any political activities, either for or against any political group. My parents, Celestino Heres, my father and my mother, Serafina, middle class merchants, were born in Spain and came to Cuba in the 1920's. My sister Mirita, my younger brother Pepe, and I were born in Cuba.

My friends and roommates at North Carolina State warned me not to go back to Cuba. They feared for my life because the political situation in Cuba was getting extremely tense. The guerillas of Fidel Castro and Ernesto "Che" Guevara were making progress against the Batista regime, and the people of Cuba were leaning towards a revolution. My sympathies, as well as the sympathies of many of my friends in the United States, were for the revolution, and we would have loved to have a democratic government in Cuba. Some of my closest friends at N.C State, among them, two United States Marines from Camp Lejeune and three paratroopers from the 82nd Airborne Division stationed at Fort Bragg, even volunteered to help me. They planned to arrange for a cache of weapons to be sent to Cuba in the fight against Fulgencio Batista. After years of listening to my friends and roommates discussing the American Civil War over beers in front of our apartment fireplace, you could believe that they were serious about the weapons. Of course, I did not want any part of it. All I wanted to do was to go home to my dear family and childhood friends; however, in my heart, I wanted freedom of the press and free elections for Cuba. To see Batista deposed and a democracy in power would have been in the best interests of Cuba and its populace. One early Saturday morning, Sergeant David McCloud, a marine from Camp Lejeune who had come to visit us, was bringing into the kitchen several boxes of K-rations (dry beef, Spam, corned beef) when he accidentally ignited a yellow smoke hand grenade canister. With an uncanny speed, he threw the grenade out the window on to Hillsboro Street, a main thoroughfare in Raleigh. The smoke covered a large area, from the front of our house to the Memorial Tower of N.C. State. I never thought this canister could generate such a large screen of yellow smoke. The police never found out who had done this, but then there was always friction between the students and the police. Since we were always short of cash, it was nice to have the food we got from the marines and paratroopers. They brought this food as a gift to us for letting them stay and sleep in our house over the weekends and participate in our parties. To this day, I cannot eat these foods and especially not on top of a toast, which is known by a very peculiar name by people in the military.

In August 1958, as I boarded a National Airlines plane in Miami, I had no idea of the events that I was going to be a part of when I arrived in Cuba. I landed at the Havana airport and took the bus. After about an hour's ride, I arrived at my hometown of Colón, which I had left three and a half years before. It never ceased to amaze me how

The Reluctant Revolutionary in Raleigh, N.C
1958

beautiful the Cuban countryside was, especially the abundance of royal palm trees swaying in the tropical breeze, the beautiful "framboyanes" with their orange blossoms and the contrast of its green color vegetation against the fabulous blue skyline. When I reached my home, suitcases loaded with presents for my brother, my sister, my parents, and my friends, I was truly traumatized. Instead of a glorious welcome, I saw my parents and sister embracing each other and crying. It took me awhile to calm them down, and, although they were very happy to see me, they had other things much more important with which to cope. Finally, they calmed down enough to talk and explain to me that my younger brother, Pepito, only 16 years old, had decided to join the revolution. Pepito had left home with some of our best childhood friends and headed for the Escambray Mountains.

They had gone searching for Comandante Rolando Cubela, a friend of mine from my years at La Progresiva, a top-notch high school managed by the Presbyterian Church, where my friends and I developed a love for democracy. If Pepito and his friends could not find Cubela they were going to look for Che, the Argentinean doctor and intimate friend of Raul and Fidel Castro, who was also in hiding in the Escambray Mountains. The location of these mountains was extremely important because from there a group of revolutionaries could move across Cuba from north to south and cut the island in half, thereby cutting off supplies and material needed by Batista's troops and guaranteeing the end of Batista's regime.

I could not believe, that my younger brother, Pepito, who, like me, was not a fanatic, had actually joined a political group. I had expressed to him my sentiments that life is too precious to sacrifice it for some unknown person to obtain power and later betray you. We had talked about Hitler, Mussolini, Stalin, Franco, and others who had betrayed their followers. Many loyal men had sacrificed their lives for nothing. The only motivation these dictators had was to satisfy their egos and to advance their ambitions. In the end, they are remembered as traitors to their cause and recognized not as heroes but as failures.

Although my brother was younger than I, he was very mature for his age, and I thought I understood him well. Of course, my first thought was that his friends had influenced him. I was not aware of the passion of the situation in Cuba, that most of our friends had joined the revolution, and that most were in the Escambray. What happened next was to have a great impact in my life. My childhood friend Rolando Gonzalez, who we called "Palillo", or " Toothpick", because he was so skinny, was chief of sabotage in our region in charge of destroying electrical and telegraphic lines. With his approval, I decided to search for my brother. Even though all of the local leaders told me that it was senseless to go after him in an area as large as the Escambray, as a teenager, I had explored the Escambray Mountains and knew about certain passes one had to cross if one wanted to get anywhere. Based on this recollection, I went home, put on heavy-duty clothing and hiking boots, grabbed my army compass, and filled my backpack with as many provisions as I could carry (cans of tuna, crackers, peanut butter, cereal bars, etc). Later that night, at about one o'clock in the morning, five friends who wanted to join the revolution and I who only wanted to find my brother took off for the mountains.

We evaded one of the many blockades, some with up to five hundred troops, that Batista's army had set up in the interior, and proceeded to penetrate deep into the mountains. After two days of difficult walking and climbing, we finally joined a group of rebels who welcomed us. They enjoyed some of our provisions and asked what our plans were. I explained my desire to find my brother, and they replied that anyone who wished to join the revolutionary group must go to the headquarters of Comandante

Cubela; since they were going in that direction they told us to follow them.

We walked for what seemed days rather than hours and finally reached Cubela's forest encampment. As I entered the field tent, to my amazement there was my brother, Pepito. Sitting next to my brother was Che Guevara, smoking a large Cuban cigar. My brother and I embraced and jumped with joy. After this ecstatic reunion, I proceeded to give him hell for what he had done. I explained how devastated our parents were, and asked what was the meaning of smoking a cigar in front of me, something he had never done before. Everybody laughed at my comments and one of Che's soldiers remarked that the only reason Che was sitting with my brother was that Pepito had brought some cigars with him and Che could not resist a good cigar. So, it was not fate that brought us together but a Cuban cigar.

This was my first contact with the famous Che, a skinny, ill- looking character, who was racked with a chronic cough. He suffered from asthma and the humid mountain air was of no help to him, especially since it had been raining torrents on and off for three days. He proceeded to congratulate my brother for his heroic decision to join the revolution at its most important moment and to becoming a "guerrillero" like himself. From the beginning I could perceive Che's charisma. Despite Che Guevara's outward appearance, he was a tiger, a la Emiliano Zapata; any man would be glad to go into battle with him.

My only thought at that moment was how to get back home as soon as possible. But, I sensed that we were too deeply committed, and it was going to be a long time before I would see my parents again. I wished I had brought some cigars with me. Maybe we could have persuaded Che to let us return home, but in those days I did not have an appreciation for Cuban cigars. In reality, it was wishful thinking; Che would never have allowed us to return to Colón, cigar or no cigar. Che knew that we were all students from good families and not connected in any way to Batista's government. When Che mentioned my schooling at North Carolina in the United States, I sensed from him a bit of mistrust. I wished my brother had not told him anything about me. I had mentioned to Che that I always had kept a photo of Fidel Castro on top of our fireplace back in North Carolina. To be honest, while studying at the university my sympathies were with the revolution…from a distance. I had heard a rumor that Fidel Castro was a communist, but in those days I didn't want to believe it. All I cared about was that he was fighting against the dictator Batista. I was not totally ignorant about communism, having taken an undergraduate course on Marxism-Leninism. I knew that communism as an economic doctrine was a real disaster, that the creativity of the individual was destroyed, and that becoming dependent on the government would make people lazy with no desire to compete and better themselves. In any event, here I was, far from the peaceful North Carolina State campus in the midst of a revolutionary force bent on deposing Batista. I had found Pepito, but, unfortunately, the revolution had found me.

Che

Chapter Two: The Train

In the many days that followed, I had the opportunity to talk to Che Guevara about politics, but he never for one instant tried to convert me to his ideas. As a matter of fact, I had trouble finding out what his actual ideas were. In the early days of the revolution nobody talked about communism, and the only talk was about democracy, freedom of expression, and freedom of the press. This was what we were supposed to be fighting for. I did hear a great deal about the United States policy to support dictators, that Cuba was never a free country and was always dependent on the American government. I heard comments about the Platt Amendment which gave the United States the right to intervene in Cuban affairs at any time and how our national territory was violated by having to give up Guantanamo for an

American naval base. What seemed to hurt Che and his followers the most was the fact that the United States government did not allow our leaders who had fought in the Independence War to travel to France to sign the Treaty of Paris, which concluded what they called "the Cuban-Spanish-American War." Cubans fought the Spanish army for thirty years and deserved to sign the treaty too. At that time, this kind of talk meant nothing to me. I did not join the revolution on my free will; I was a reluctant revolutionary, and I wanted to go home. Besides, I definitely was not anti-American, nor were most Cubans.

Our days of leisure in the mountains did not last very long. Word was received that Batista's army was demoralized: soldiers designated to drive trucks to the front, loaded with gasoline, had been seen selling their cargo to private gasoline stations for their own personal profit, and many soldiers were deserting their posts after receiving their pay.

Our revolutionary group began to grow to over 400 men. It was relatively well armed, and was eager to come out of the mountains and fight. We received information from our forward units that an armored train loaded with weapons and ammunition, sent by dictator Trujillo of the Dominican Republic and a friend of Batista, was coming towards the city of Santa Clara. Che and the other comandantes became very excited and saw this as an opportunity to obtain more and better weapons and get ready for what we knew was the primary objective: to take over the city of Santa Clara thereby cutting the island in half. This would allow Castro and his group, now in the Oriente province, to march westward towards us and, eventually, to the city of Havana, the ultimate objective.

I am afraid that I got caught by the emotions of the moment, and for the first time, even with butterflies in my stomach, I wanted to participate in this crazy enterprise. The thought that my brother and I could get killed brought me back to reality, but the adrenaline and the spirit of young people got hold of us and, finally, we officially joined the revolution. I was amazed at the valuable information we were receiving from our spies concerning the time and route of the armored train. We marched towards the site of our planned ambush, positioned ourselves, and waited for whatever was going to happen. I could not believe that we were going to attack an armored train. I wondered, "How does one fight with only small caliber guns, pistols, a few hand grenades, and an occasional bazooka against such a fortified train?"

I expected the train to come barreling through our ambush site and pass us at full speed all the while shooting at us. Military strategy not being one of my best skills, I could not think of a feasible way to attack this train. Finally, Che came over and explained his strategy. Some of our people would remove tracks ahead of the train to bring it to a halt and then tracks would be removed from the back of the train and, Bingo! The "super" armored train would become a sitting duck, and more than that, a wounded sitting duck. My God! This seemed crazy to me! Batista's soldiers would come out of the train and massacre us. Besides, I thought, there must be additional troops stationed nearby who would come to the rescue of the train. I was in a state of panic and hoped my face would not give my emotions away.

As it turned out, the train not only carried weapons and munitions but also hundreds of Batista's soldiers. We also knew that some of the soldiers in that train were criminals who had tortured and murdered some of our friends, and, surely, they would not allow us to capture them. At this moment I was armed with a Colt .45 automatic revolver, a Thompson submachine gun, a few hand grenades, and a bowie knife, which I had brought all the way from a shop in North Carolina. This knife was the only weapon I brought with me when I took off to find my brother; now, I guess, I would have been considered as a "heavily armed" revolutionary. My brother, Pepito, was armed with a shotgun, a revolver, and a few hand grenades. Again I thought, "How can we fight with these weapons against an armored train?"

We waited for the train to make its appearance. After what I thought was a very long time, we heard the tremendous noise generated by the monstrous locomotive engine and saw in the distance the large, gray enemy, which contained enough firepower to kill us all. As it passed by us, my heart pounded when I saw its daunting size. To my amazement, the train came to a sudden stop right in front of where our group had set up the ambush. Oddly, there was no shooting from inside the train, and there were no gunshots or machine gun fire from any of our men. Obviously, the train had to stop because there were no more tracks, and when it began to back-up, the engineer was told that there were no tracks to back up either. The expression "sitting duck" was absolutely correct in this case. There was no place to go but to sit there. All of a sudden there was absolute silence all around us. I have never heard a silence as silent and foreboding as this one. There was no shooting, nobody spoke, and the gray mass of the armored train just sat there. I expected soldiers to come out shooting because by this time I knew they could see us. "Pretty soon we would all be dead," I thought. But nothing happened.

"What will be next?" I asked myself. Che's Machiavellian plan was incredible. Out of nowhere came a truck with loudspeakers, like the ones used to announce sales through the streets of my hometown or during political rallies. Driving the truck was Pachiro, a friend of mine, who was in the broadcast business, and, after positioning the truck, he began to play the Cuban national anthem. After the anthem ended, he proceeded to encourage the soldiers to surrender. He announced over the loudspeakers that the officers could keep their weapons, that they would be welcome to join us in our great historical moment, and so on. While this was going on, I kept thinking about David and Goliath: we David, they Goliath. This went on for about two hours until finally a side door of one of the cars opened and an officer of Batista's army came out to talk to us. He communicated that they were willing to surrender under the already announced provision, that the officers would be allowed to keep their weapons and that the soldiers were to be given the option of either going home or joining us. After this was agreed to and the officer returned to the car, other doors opened and a large number of unarmed young soldiers began to exit the train.

Suddenly we heard shots coming from inside one of the cars, and I thought this was it. I thought that we were being betrayed and we would have no choice but to engage in the fighting. What happened was that the wanted men inside had decided that they would commit suicide rather than face execution by some of the members of Che's men, who had a long list of what they called "war criminals."

After this scare, everything proceeded in an orderly fashion. Many young soldiers joined our group, as well as some of the officers. My brother and I entered the armored train, and my eyes could not believe the large number of weapons, boxes of grenades, boxes of dynamite, bazookas and ordnance of all kinds.

I said to myself that with all these weapons we should be able to attack and defeat the military headquarters in the city of Santa Clara. Che was beside himself when he saw all these weapons and kept saying, "Now we will have the upper hand!" His remarks about going to fight in Santa Clara did not make me feel any better. Up until now, things had been relatively easy, but I felt that Santa Clara would be another story.

Chapter Three: The Battle for Santa Clara

Before we could attack Santa Clara we had to take the city of Cabaiguan. Our forward group had already reported to us that the Cabaiguan garrison was very demoralized and the soldiers there were ready to run away and abandon their posts. In spite of this intelligence, we entered Cabaiguan with great care, and we were lucky that we did. Our intelligence turned out to be completely wrong; there was some fighting and four men in our group were killed. We noticed that some of Batista's younger soldiers had run away, and, more importantly, I was able to verify that the drivers of the super gasoline tanker trucks were still selling their contents to local gasoline dealers. I knew this meant that the gasoline designated for the army's tanks and trucks would not be available. We would be able to take advantage of this and, hopefully, win the fight against Batista. I then found out that the bridges connecting the towns of Cabaiguan, Trinidad, and Sancti Spiritus had been blown out. The fact that these three bridges had been destroyed made me feel a bit more relaxed because it looked like things were starting to turn in our favor again.

We took Cabaiguan on December 23 and then moved towards Santa Clara. If we could take this key city, we could cut the island in half, and then Fidel and his people could come from the Oriente province to join us. Three of our columns began to enter the city of Santa Clara. Unfortunately, my column had one of the worst times. Before we even approached the city, we were attacked by air. Several 500-pound bombs, delivered by B-26's, fell very near us, and I saw the roofs of several buildings blown away. We each had to cut a piece of soft wood, hang it from a piece of string that we tied around our necks, and bite it so as to prevent the concussion from making us bleed from the nose and ears. Fortunately, not long after the initial air attack, either the planes ran out of fuel or ran out of bombs because they did not come back. I also had a suspicion that Batista's pilots were defecting.

As my brother and I entered a narrow street we saw an amazing   surreal picture. A priest carrying a white flag was arguing with an officer begging him not to destroy his small church, which had been built in the 16th Century. Evidently, the priest quickly lost the argument because a moment later a Sherman tank approached the church and headed straight into it.   The tank bulldozed the church entering from the front to the back, destroying everything in its path. I saw prayer books, and hymns books flying in the air. I also noticed that after he had lost the argument with the officer and saw his church being destroyed, the priest began shooting at the soldiers with a machine gun. I learned later that this priest had acquired his knowledge of automatic weapons during the Spanish Civil War.

As the tank exited from the back of the church carrying and dragging pieces of benches and articles from the main altar, I watched my brother and two of my friends attempting to disable the tank by shooting at it with their shotguns. Talk about David and Goliath! Were they crazy trying to fight a tank with only shotguns?

But then, as the tank veered to the right into another narrow street trying to avoid the shotgun fire which, in reality, could have injured the driver's eyes, I heard a loud explosion. All of a sudden, in front of my very eyes, this Sherman tank just blew up. It actually was propelled a couple of feet from the ground. Now I understood the reason for the shotguns. Their goal had been to attract the tank down the street where the explosives had been placed. When the tank passed over a hole, the dynamite was detonated destroying the tank and killing everyone inside.

As the battle concluded, we didn't know that Batista had sent reinforcements, and the garrison in Santa Clara consisted now of 3,500 soldiers and was commanded by Colonel Joaquin Casillas. This colonel did not know that we had already captured the armored train, whose supplies were needed to defend his garrison. On December 29, Che Guevara broadcast from radio station CMQ in the University of Santa Clara area into the deepest parts of the center of the city. He was announcing to the populace that the revolution had started and was asking the people to actively support the revolution against Batista. Many civilians joined us with Molotov cocktails they had prepared. Over the next three days, the city of Santa Clara turned into a bloody struggle. I had never seen so many dead people as a result of intense house-to-house fighting.

Late in the afternoon on December 29 we made great progress. Our own "suicide squad" took the train station. Batista's soldiers ran for the protection of the armored train, not realizing that we had captured it.

The suicide squad, commanded by "El Vaquerito," Roberto Rodriguez, was an insane group of fanatic admirers of Che. As a newcomer to Che's group I was glad that I was not yet trusted enough to join this suicide squad. But, my brother, Pepe, young and possessing the usual belief of the young that he would live forever, wanted to join in. It was a good thing that I was there to persuade him not to. He would not have survived the attack, as many did not. If there was ever a time we could have used those yellow smoke grenades from Raleigh, the time was now. It could have saved a good number of lives. We were part of 340 fighters commanded by Che, together with about 100 men from Comandante Cubela's Directorio.

All of a sudden, we came under intense machine-gun fire and hit the ground real hard. It was then that I saw Che in front of me screaming in pain. I was sure that he had been shot when I saw him holding up his right elbow. Then I realized that he had fractured the elbow area on his left arm when he had hit the dirt to avoid the machine-gun fire. We took him inside the first house we saw and had a lucky break. Dr. Oscar Fernandez Mell, a resident of my hometown, a childhood friend, and one of Che's trusted comandantes, was inside and proceeded to make a splint and cast.

After Che's arm was set, we continued the battle. The three columns finally joined and proceeded with the mop-up operations. We took several tanks, jeeps, and trucks, which we later used in our march to Havana, our final objective. I have to say that I was immensely happy to see the end of this hard fought battle. I turned to Che to congratulate him and found him looking very sad. I thought that maybe it was the pain from his fracture, but then I realized that he was only happy when the fighting was going on. I sensed that he would have been happier if the fighting had gone on forever. This was exactly the opposite of my sentiments; I was delighted to see the end of this lunacy.

Che after the battle for Santa Clara

Chapter Four: The Road to Havana

On the morning of January 2, our group, directed by Che and Camilo Cienfuegos, proposed that we should march forward to Havana as soon as possible. There was fear that other organizations were ready to take over the government. My brother, our Colón friends, and I climbed into one of the trucks we had captured together, and, much to my relief, I realized we were going to pass through Colón, located along the central highway in Cuba, on our way to Havana.

It is very strange that all the time I was part of this adventure, I had no idea as to what was going on in the Oriente province or in the rest of the island. I assumed that our victory was total and that Fidel Castro, Raul, and the others would join us in our march to Havana. Prior to my return to Cuba I had been isolated at North Carolina State. Even though there were excellent local newspapers in Raleigh, they published very little as to what was actually going on in Cuba. Besides, I was too preoccupied coping with my engineering studies, the parties, and my friends to worry about Cuban politics.

When everything was in place, we starting moving towards Havana. I had the opportunity to phone my mother before leaving Santa Clara. Surprisingly, the telephones were working, at least the line between Santa Clara and Colón. My mother was very excited and relieved when she discovered for the first time since our departures that Pepito and I were alive and well. She got so nervous that she hung up the phone before I had an opportunity to speak with my father. Later, I was told that after I talked to her she went right to her sewing machine and started to sew two flags: one Cuban flag and another, a red and black flag with a star in the center, which represented the revolutionary flag of the "Movement 26 of July," Fidel Castro's organization. The name "26 of July" was derived from Castro's attack on the Moncada garrison in Oriente province, which marked the beginning of the struggle against the dictator Fulgencio Batista.

After we left Santa Clara, to continue our journey in preparation for our assault on Havana, we were delayed several times by the people in the different towns on the way there, like: Esperanza, Jicotea, Santo Domingo, Cascajal, and Los Arabos. The locals brought us cigars, cigarettes, water, beer, and even something to eat. I was surprised at my lack of appetite. Since I had left home I had lost at least thirty pounds, and my brother

Cuban and "26 of July Movement" flags

looked like a bag of bones. But now, a simple ham sandwich tasted terrific and a glass of milk tasted like honey.

Finally, we approached my hometown of Colón, and there on the sidewalk were my mother, father and sister holding up the two flags my mother had sewn. I also noticed that many people were wearing red and black armbands in support of the revolution. The people of Colón had always actively participated in our quest for freedom, and, in every historical endeavor, there was always someone from our town involved. For example, Doctor Mario Muñoz, a family friend, was killed in the Moncada attack, Castro's first military effort. The doctor was married to a beautiful woman, had a lovely daughter, and had a successful medical practice. Another good friend of my family,

Jose Echevarria, was killed in the attack on the Presidential Palace. Jose had broadcast from a radio station in Havana and then blew it up when he got off the air. Batista's police had killed him afterward. How could anybody with the nickname of "Manzanita" ("Little Apple") because of his red cheeks, commit such an attack? He was the son of a wealthy family and a student leader at the University of Havana. I personally knew these two people, and I would never have guessed in a million years that they would be involved in such violent activities. I guess they were also reluctant revolutionaries.

We must have looked terrible because our parents had trouble recognizing us. My brother and I had on green fatigues, wore religious medals given to us by friends, and sported our wooden mouthpieces, which were still dangling from around our necks since the air attack on Santa Clara. I was wearing a beret, Pepito an olive green military cap.

We came down off the truck and kissed and embraced our parents and sister; we had always been a loving and touching family. Somebody announced that we had to continue our march towards Havana and that nobody was to remain behind. I was already back home where I wanted to stay, but now I had no choice. At this moment something bizarre happened. My poor father was so excited when he saw us that he tripped over a piece of wood on the sidewalk and fell to the ground. He had broken his right leg. Again, luck intervened, and Dr. Oscar Fernandez Mell just happened to be there when this accident occurred. We took my father in Dr. Mell's jeep to a clinic nearby to have his leg xrayed. After the x-rays were taken Doctor Mell proceeded to set my father's leg while we laughed at the thought that the same doctor who set Che's elbow was doing the same to my father's leg. We also talked about how I had saved his life during an ambush in Santa Clara and he was very thankful.

We took my father home, laid him on his bed, and kissed both of our parents goodbye; my brother and I then climbed back into Dr. Mell's jeep and proceeded to join the column marching towards Havana. We arrived at Camp Columbia late in the afternoon and secured the place. We had no problems and quickly accommodated ourselves. We then began to wait for Fidel and Raul Castro and their men.

I did not have enough time to bathe or shave my beard while in Colón, but now I was finally able to take a shower. However, I was not permitted to shave. I guess the comandantes decided that for public relations purposes the beards had become a status symbol they would like to preserve. I also realized that this was what distinguished us from the rest of the military and others who came into Camp Columbia. Our beards had become badges of honor and it was thought to be sacrilegious to shave them. I was also ordered to keep my weapons with me at all times.

I learned that there was friction between Comandante Cubela and Che. Cubela did not want to give up his independent status and, specifically, did not want to do anything with the communist cells in Che's group. This may show how gullible I was at that time, but this was the first time I recognized the possibility of communists among our group. There was little or no talk at all about the communist influence in our groups. Our main objective had always been to remove the dictator Batista from power and establish a democratic government in Cuba. Innocent as I was, I once said, "We can always get rid of any communist attempt to take power." I did not know that our great leader, Fidel Castro, had strong communist sentiments, and little did I imagine what was going to follow later.

When Che was sent to occupy the Cabaña Fortress, I thought this was done to keep the communists from the limelight. Comandante Camilo Cienfuego, the best of all the comandantes, was to be in charge of Camp Columbia, where my brother and I had found accommodations.

I found out that Fidel was now entering the City of Santiago de Cuba, in Oriente province, close to the mountains where Fidel Castro had spent most of the time. From Santiago, Fidel slowly began making his way towards Havana. My friends told me that Fidel thoroughly enjoyed the adoration of the crowds. The country received him and his group as heroes. Meanwhile, we had trouble in Havana. Even though Batista's remaining soldiers were in their barracks and had surrendered after Batista's flight to the Dominican Republic and then to the Island of Madeira on New Year's Day, 1959, we had some sniper fire directed at us, and, by God, I thought this time I was going to get it. Fortunately, my brother and his group found the snipers and killed them. This was my last experience under fire, and it made me even more reluctant to be a revolutionary.

When Comandante Camilo Cienfuegos saw me, he invited my brother and me to join the Revolutionary Directory and to move with his group into the Presidential Palace. We accepted; I thought I would rather be in the Presidential Palace than in the military camp of Columbia. I felt safer with Camilo who, to tell the truth, had facial features that reminded me of the picture of Jesus Christ that my mother always kept hanging up in her bedroom. Che came to talk to Camilo, and he looked very unhappy about Camilo taking over the Presidential Palace.

When Fidel Castro finally arrived in Havana, I had already encountered President Manuel Urrutia, the man Fidel had chosen as his front man. At first President Urrutia did not recognized me. After I told him who I was and that I knew he had once been a judge in Colón, he remembered me. He and his wife Alejandra and their two children, Alejandrito and Adolfito, lived in an apartment that my father built directly above our home. As a child I used to play with Alejandrito, and I remember how captivated I was by the beauty and intelligence of Alejandra, his mother. President Urrutia asked me about my parents, and we established a cordial relationship. I found out that his personal security officer, who was also present, was none other than my hometown pharmacist, Ismael Martinez, father of my dearest and best friend, Jorge, who lived two doors away from my home. Jorge was forced to leave for the United States because the Havana police were after him. He never returned to Cuba. Ismael took me aside and confided to me how unhappy he was with what Fidel was doing to Urrutia, using him as the scapegoat for all of Fidel's problems. I carefully told him not to repeat this opinion to anybody else for his own safety.

On January 8 Fidel finally arrived at the Presidential Palace. At last, I was to meet the great "Barbudo," the bearded one, the father of the glorious revolution, the "maximum" leader. He arrived on top of a captured Sherman tank, and I found his arrival rather comical, more like a maharajah riding on an Indian elephant than a great political leader arriving in triumph. When he alit from the tank and entered the Palace he greeted me. The only reason Fidel acknowledged me at all was because I was in the company of Urrutia and Camilo; otherwise, he would not have even looked at me. I mentioned to Fidel that I was from Colón, a neighbor of Dr. Oscar Fernandez Mell, and was with Che in Santa Clara when he broke his elbow. I don't know how much he really knew about me, but the fact that I was in the battle of Santa Clara was enough for him to at least trust me. Afterwards, I learned that he knew everything about me and knew everything about everyone in that room. He knew of my schooling in North Carolina, of the search for my brother, and every move I had made since reaching the Escambray Mountains up to the moment he set eyes on me. He even knew about my fiancée whom I had met when we were students in the United States and my desire to get married as soon as I graduated. Fidel would never be surrounded by anybody who had not been previously checked out. Up to this moment, I thought that my sweetheart, Elsa, her parents, and mine were the only people who knew about our future marital plans.

That night Fidel spoke on radio to the nation. His speech hypnotized everybody present in the broadcasting booth and all of those listening on radio and watching him on television. This was the first time the nation saw him with his fatigue uniform, looking like a guerrilla fighter.

The next morning, my good luck continued. I was asked to disband and return to my home in Colón. I later learned that the Revolutionary Directorate I had joined when reaching Havana was the first group asked to disarm and disband. I did not turn in my weapons but decided to take them home with me. Sometimes simple decisions come back to haunt you; this simple decision to keep my weapons turned out to be a major mistake.

Chapter Five: Colón, Raleigh, N.C., and Havana

The minute I got home, I began to talk about getting back to North Carolina and completing my engineering degree. I found some resistance to my plans from the new people who were placed in charge of running my hometown. They were members of Fidel's "Movement 26 of July Organization," mostly farmers, unemployed people, and general nobodies before the revolution. They resented the fact that I was educated and strongly suggested that I returned to Havana to ask Fidel's permission to leave Cuba. To this day I have kept the letter of authorization to leave Cuba which states that I should return to Cuba no later than August of 1959. Since I was planning to get married in August upon my return, I was happy to oblige. Fidel wanted me to return with my education completed so as to work for the better future of Cuba. It was at this time that Fidel gave me an autographed photograph of himself with a telescopic rifle. I felt a heavy weight on my back when he said: "This is so that you won't forget us."

The reality that my family had never been involved with Batista and was respected by everyone was a great asset to me. The fact that Fidel's father was from Galicia, the province adjoining Asturias, my father's home province in Spain, did not hurt either. I had mentioned to Fidel that the Asturians started the reconquest of Spain and helped to defeat and expel the Arabs from Spain; as a result, we were now speaking Spanish and not Arabic. Anyway, I received official permission to leave Cuba and immediately returned to Raleigh. I was full of ideology and enthusiasm about subsequently returning to Cuba to work for elections, the free press, and a true democracy.

Before returning to N.C. State, I visited the Marrero Brothers' barbershop and experienced the great pleasure of a Cuban shave. Before removing my beard, Ramon Marrero placed hot towels on my face, shaved me with a straight razor, cleaned my face with several creams, and finished with an ice pack to close the pores. Now I was ready for the world.

Soon after I returned to Raleigh, I invited some members of the new Revolutionary Cuban Diplomatic Corp to come to the University of North Carolina to speak about the great plans we had for a new Cuba, a Cuba free of American influence, a true nationalistic nation. I even felt that the United States should be allowed to keep their military base on Cuban soil in Guantanamo, even though this American military base had been a thorn in the hearts of many Cubans. I had no anti-American feelings; I loved the United States and its people. I just did not appreciate the United States government's policy towards military dictators.

The newspapers in North Carolina were replete with negative articles about the revolution in Cuba and especially against Fidel Castro. From day one, the editorials continued to accuse him of being a communist. I kept saying to myself that this was impossible, and I even went on the radio in Wilson, North Carolina, to defend Fidel and everything he did and stood for. How can he be a communist, our "Robin Hood," who came from the mountains to defeat the dictator? I was there when the revolution happened; I saw everything firsthand, and I did not considered myself a communist.

I did not want to see a government in Cuba like the one in the Soviet Union. I also knew about the Korean War and the Iron Curtain in Europe, but my philosophical understanding of Marxism-Leninism came mostly from the books and articles I had read and an introductory course on communism I had taken. Besides, if communism was truly bad, the people of Cuba could defeat it as we had defeated Batista. How gullible was I at that time!

At last, June came around, and I graduated from North Carolina State University; I knew that my parents would be so proud. I was the first in my family, a family whose history dated back to the year 718 A.D., to graduate from college, and from a top American institution to boot. I could hardly wait to go back home, but at the same time I was experiencing strong feelings of regret and sorrow about leaving behind so many great friends that I had made while studying in Raleigh. I packed my things, bought a bottle of Johnny Walker Black for my father and a carton of Lucky Strikes for my mother, said goodbye to all my professors and dear friends, and took the flight from Raleigh to Miami to Havana.

The flight from Miami to Havana started very positively; the stewardess was very generous offering us frozen daiquiris. I felt very relaxed and happy that I was finally going home to my family, fiancée, and friends. Shortly after takeoff, the captain announced that we would be landing at the airport in Havana. I took a good look out the window anxious to see my beloved Cuba again. Then, as we flew over Havana harbor, what did I see? Two huge ships flying the flag of the Soviet Union and the sickle and hammer painted on their smokestacks. Instantly, the effects of the daiquiris left me, and I was sure that I must have turned pale, because the stewardess asked me if I was feeling sick. I was indeed feeling sick, not because of the drinks, but because I could not understand the presence of those ships in the harbor.

When the plane landed, my fiancée and her parents met me at the airport. No sooner were we in their car when they all at once began to inform me what had occurred in Cuba since my departure only five months before. They could not tell me anything specifically about the political situation over the phone when I called them from North

Carolina. They could not write anything in letters because the mail was being monitored by the Cuban authorities. So much for freedom! They told me that two of my closest friends had been executed by Che in the Cabaña Fortress, and two other childhood friends, Mongo and Pepe Garcia, had been sentenced to 25 to 30 years in prison for anti-revolutionary activities. They had been caught transporting arms to the Escambray to start fighting against Fidel and the revolution.

Elsa also told me that all of the important positions in our province and in my hometown had been assigned to members of Che's and Fidel's organizations. Most of these people came from different distant cities to avoid favoritism among the local citizens but also to eliminate any sympathy when these officials ordered the execution or imprisonment of locals. In spite of this, my father was able to walk into the headquarters of the local militia. He talked to the comandante in charge and convinced him to release a group of his friends, Jewish merchants, who had been arrested for opposing the nationalization of their businesses. Elsa did not want me to stay in Havana. She wanted us to get married and return to the United States before things got any worse.

Finally, our wedding day arrived. We got married and we went to the Island of Pines for our honeymoon. There, we stayed at the brand new Colony Hotel. I did not realize how isolated we would be from the daily events on the mainland. When we returned home to Colón after two weeks away, my father informed me that he was worried about my security since so many of my friends were in trouble with Castro's people. In addition, some members of the newly created militia were looking for me. According to my father I was supposed to have reported to Camp Columbia headquarters. He said that the comandante in charge was very upset that I had not reported immediately upon my arrival in Cuba from the United States. I had assumed that after I was demilitarized and had left for the United States to complete my education that my responsibilities towards the revolution had concluded. I was just expecting a civilian position, in some engineering capacity. Evidently, I was wrong. They had different plans for me.

My next disappointment had to do with freedom of the press. I noticed that whenever the revolutionary government did not agree with an editorial or an article in the newspaper, a disclaimer would appear below the article stating the government's official position on the issue and sometimes even making fun of the article. To me, this was nothing else but a form of censorship. Once again, the changing political times would affect my personal and now my married life.

Chapter Six: Showdown with Fidel Castro

The time finally came when I had no choice but to go to Havana and face the music. Instead of going to Camp Columbia, I decided to go directly to the Presidential Palace where I knew my friend Dr. Mell had been assigned as an advisor to Che. I wanted to talk to him because, out of all my friends, he was the closest confidante of Che and Fidel. I wanted to find out what was really going on now and what those in power had in store for the future of Cuba. I did not realize how foolish I was by going into the "lion's lair" without a whip and a chair. I guess this time I was not as reluctant to get involved as I was at the beginning. In reality, I think I was angry at the current developments in Cuba. My wife was totally opposed to my decision to go to Havana and had advised me to go into hiding and wait until I had time to talk to those close friends who had accompanied me to the Escambray Mountains. My brother, Pepito, was working in Varadero, running a nightclub for the government and was totally out of the political loop. In spite of Elsa's advice, I went to Havana.

As I climbed the steps of the Presidential Palace and reached the room where I expected to find my friend Dr. Mell alone, much to my surprise, Fidel, Raul, Che, Dr. Mell, and others were talking loudly, the way we Cubans have a tendency to speak. They all turned around to see me come in. I was welcomed with, "It was about time you showed up!" from one of them, but I couldn't tell who. I quickly replied, smiling and joking, that a newly married man needs time for his honeymoon. Not to my surprise, Raul Castro gruffly stated that the country comes before one's personal life. I wanted to reply that perhaps my hormones were stronger than his. It was a good thing that I kept my mouth shut this time, but I did not keep it shut for very long.

I proceeded to make my first mistake. I mentioned that as I was flying over Havana's harbor, I was very surprised to see two ships from the Soviet Union. I asked Fidel about them, and he said, "We are having a real democracy in Cuba and we are going to allow all ideologies to participate in the new revolutionary government." My second mistake was to tell Fidel that communism is like a cancer, once it gets into your finger, it will eat your arm and then your whole body. All of a sudden, an extraordinary silence fell all over the room. If there had been a fly on the table you probably could have heard its wings moving. Fidel looked me in the eye and said, "Your problem is that you do not have a true revolutionary mind." At that moment I remembered having been given a photograph of Fidel holding a telescopic rifle with the inscription, "To my friend from Colón, Tino Heres, a true revolutionary." I said, "Fidel, make up your mind; am I a true revolutionary or not?" I do not know where I got the courage to say this, but Fidel's eyes became so cold that I thought the air in the room was going to turn to ice. Dr. Mell tried to change the topic of the conversation, but the anger in me forced me to continue. I asked about the timeline for elections, and when the Cuban people were finally going to have the opportunity to elect our candidates democratically. Fidel responded adamantly, "We don't need elections! We are a true

Fidel Castro with telescopic rifle

revolutionary government of the people! They love us and we don't need elections!" Having heard his statement, "We don't need elections" twice gave me the courage to continue. But, before I could say anything, Fidel interrupted me and said, "We must complete the work of the revolution: have an agrarian reform, change the monetary system, and bring balance to this society. There will be time for elections later."

Full of courage, I replied, "Fidel, many of us who participated in the revolution did it in order to bring free elections to Cuba, freedom of the press, and respect for human rights. On this last issue I think we are already failing by executing those who disagree with your ideas." From the corner of my eye I could see Che Guevara's face turning red. I thought Dr. Mell was going to faint from the way he looked at me. As I mentioned before, there was already censorship of the press. It really bothered me that Fidel and the others believed that <u>El Diario de la Marina</u>, a Catholic controlled newspaper, was printing lies against the revolutionary government. Fidel and his people thought that the owners of <u>El Diario</u> and other newspapers were reactionaries, rich people who still had sympathies towards Batista's government. That is why every time the censors objected to a specific article they the revolutionaries would add a note rebutting it.

So, after a few hours at the Presidential Palace, without President Urrutia's presence, I was told that there would be no free elections, no freedom of the press, and no relief of the abuses of human rights.

When I realized that it was futile to talk sense to Fidel, his brother, and Che, I excused myself and exited as soon as I could. My knees were shaking as I walked down the long, white, marble steps of the Presidential Palace staircase, not from fear but from anger. I heard steps behind me. When I turned, I saw my friend Dr. Mell. He held my arm and said in an intense voice: "You saved my life once in Santa Clara, and I advise you to call your wife, go to the American Embassy, and get out of Cuba as soon as possible. Ask your wife to pack and meet you there. Your life is in great danger and so is mine for telling you this. Goodbye, my friend." Those were the last words I ever heard from Dr. Mell himself.

Chapter Seven: Escape from Cuba

As soon as I called my wife, she proceeded to meet me at the American Embassy with only three suitcases, some containing our newly received wedding presents. The Embassy officers were very supportive because, after they heard some of our story, they knew that our lives were in great danger. They even called the American Ambassador to meet with us and listen to our predicament. Fortunately, both my wife and I had been students in the United States, my wife at the University of Virginia and I at North Carolina State University. Unbelievably, all of our personal records concerning our past and present were on file at the Embassy, and when an officer showed the documents to me I learned things about myself of which I had not even been aware. Once more, the record of my parents' honesty, hard work and the recommendation of people who had known me all my life were tremendous assets. The people at the American Embassy learned what kind of people we really were. They understood the urgency of our request to leave Cuba immediately, and they were indeed surprised when they saw us coming in with our suitcases, which we had left at the front desk, so as not to call too much attention.

When my wife and I were students in the United States and she visited me in Raleigh, I introduced her to my professors. While we were discussing our future career plans with them, they suggested that we should try to get entry-level teaching positions at the University and that they would be willing to help us obtain employment. Remembering this, I asked the Embassy official to call N.C. State, talk to the Dean who had offered us these positions, and to see if he was still interested in hiring us. I was not at all surprised when, after a few minutes, the Embassy official told us that N.C. State was going to accept us as members of the faculty and a cable to that effect was in the process of being sent to the Immigration Office. What transpired meant that instead of political asylum being offered to us, we would be coming to the United States as legal residents. At that time, I could have cared less what status was given to us, as long as we could get out of Cuba immediately.

Next, we were checked by the Embassy physician, our pictures were taken, and we received our green cards thereby making us legal residents of the United States. I remember that the official said to us that we would be able to become American citizens in five years. I laughed because I intended to return to Cuba as soon as possible. I did not think that what was going on in Cuba could last very long, and that the United States government would never allow a communist dictatorship so close to its mainland.

At the same time that these diplomatic procedures were occurring at the U.S. Embassy, something very interesting was going on in my hometown of Colón. A group of security people had gone to my home looking for me to place me under arrest. My mother told these officials that she had not seen me for weeks and had no idea of our whereabouts since we left for our honeymoon. Of course, this was not true and what she told these local officials could have gotten her into serious trouble. In truth, both my mother and father had seen me the day before, which, by the way, was the last time I ever saw my parents alive.

While the security people were in my house, they searched the house for weapons. They knew that I had not returned the arms at Camp Columbia and knew exactly what arms I had been issued. They went into my parents' bedroom and in their dresser they found what they were looking for: the Thompson machine gun, the Colt .45, the bowie knife, some bullet boxes, my compass, and other items I had carried to the Escambray. During the search of my mother's bedroom, they took the opportunity to steal my mother's cigar box filled with gold coins that she had been collecting over seventeen years. They also helped themselves to several bottles of perfume that my mother kept in her wardrobe. Luckily, these officials, these common thieves, overlooked my mother's jewelry that was hidden under some linens and blankets.

With the help of our friends at the Italian Embassy, this jewelry eventually found its way to me in the United States, together with some American dollars that my father had managed to accumulate through the years when the American dollar was on a par with the Cuban peso. My parents were never arrested and never suffered torture or disgrace under the Castro regime mostly because of their Spanish heritage but also because my brother, Pepito, managed to take very good care of them. The only despicable thing that occurred was that our family business was taken over by the government. Castro used the euphemism "nationalization," but I prefer to call it downright thievery. However, this "nationalization" happened to everyone who owned businesses and/or land in Cuba as the communists strengthened their stronghold by acquiring everything on the island.

While at the American Embassy, my wife and I heard a commotion in the office next to the one in which we were being kept until all of the paper work was in order. When we inquired as to what was going on, we were told that Celia Cruz, the very popular and beloved Cuban singer, was also applying for residence in the United States. Soon after, the Embassy officer took us to the basement, placed us in an Embassy vehicle, and drove us to the airport. There, he put us on a special plane, destination: Miami. All of this occurred without any interference by the Cuban airport agents. I understood the reason; we were considered diplomatic personnel, and as a result, we had diplomatic immunity.

We landed in Miami and were welcomed with open arms by extremely friendly U.S. custom officers. They really made us feel at home after some very harrowing experiences. Rather than feeling like refugees, we felt like legitimate immigrants coming to this country in search of a better future. Of course, this was not entirely true. In actuality we had come to the United States because our lives were in danger and we could not live under Castro's communism.

From the Miami airport, we took a taxi to the train station and boarded the famous "Silver Star" to Raleigh. I remembered the first time I traveled by train in the United States. When I arrived from Cuba, I made the innocent mistake of purchasing a ticket on a local train instead of on an express. It took me three days, with all of the local connections and delays, to make it from Miami to Raleigh. By now we knew better and took the Silver Star. When Elsa and I finally had settled down on the train I felt faint; butterflies were jumping in my stomach. I realized for the first time we were finally saved and that we did not have the fear, anxiety, and distress that we had felt while we were in Cuba. Of course, I felt sorry for having to leave my homeland, my family, and my friends. Yet, at that time I truly felt that this was only a temporary situation and that in the not too distant future, Elsa and I would be back in a free Cuba vacationing in Varadero Beach, as I had done since the day I was born. This "reluctant revolutionary" was not only reluctant but obviously very naïve to the ways of the world's politics.

Chapter Eight: The United States, Our New
Home, and a Surprise Visit

My wife and I finally settled down in Raleigh and began our careers as educators. I bought a shortwave radio and tried to keep informed about what was going on in Cuba. Not long after I purchased the radio, I heard the worst news from Cuba since I found out that Fidel Castro was going to implement a communist government. On October 28, 1959, I learned that Comandante Camilo Cienfuegos had disappeared while flying from Cabaiguan to Havana. My first thought was that Castro had ordered him killed because Camilo was definitely not a communist and, besides, Fidel had always been jealous of Camilo's popularity. Now, I was surer than ever that no one would be able to stop the Castro brothers' and Che Guevara's goal to align themselves with the Soviet Union.

Their hate for the United States was greater than I had ever suspected.

From this moment on, most of the accurate information that I received while I was at school was from some friends who were in exile in the United States, some who had even been with me in the Escambray Mountains or who were from Colón. From them I learned that Cuba had established political relations with the Soviet Union. This did not surprise me at all.

President Urrutia had been replaced by a puppet president, Osvaldo Dorticos. Urrutia had been an honest man, an anticommunist, and a patriot; however, my wife and I knew he would not have lasted long under Castro's rule. What really surprised me was to learn that Comandante Rolando Cubela continued to be loyal to Castro. I never sensed that he had been a communist sympathizer or ever had communist inclinations. I had been a high school friend of Cubela and also was with him in the Escambray Mountains.

Of all the news coming from Cuba, one fact that was omitted in many historical sources and one I consider to be of tremendous importance was the exchange of Cuban currency, which Castro imposed. All bank accounts were frozen. The amount of available cash in personal accounts was controlled, and a new paper money was issued. This had the impact of making all Cubans poor and dependent on the government. All of this was accomplished on one single weekend, so that on Friday, one was rich, and on Monday, one was poor. This occurred during the weekend of April 29-30 of 1961; in those brief two days, long, hard-

PRE - Castro Cuban Currency

$10 Cuban peso = $10 US dollars

$ 10 Cuban peso = $ 0 US dollars

earned savings were jeopardized, ready cash in larger amounts was not available, personal accounts had disappeared. Fidel Castro had control of the Cuban money system, and, in effect, he had a stranglehold on all of the Cuban people. My brother-in-law, Antonio Camacho, an executive of the Chase Manhattan Bank in Havana, helped our parents exchange some of our currency but in the long run our families lost practically everything.

During this time, my wife and I both continued our teaching in North Carolina. She was teaching Spanish, I, Mathematics. We took occasional trips to Miami to talk to our friends in exile and to buy some Cuban food such as malanga, plantains, black beans, and papayas, things that could not be found in Raleigh. I learned from my friends that something big was going on in Cuba, but nobody could give me one concrete bit of information as to what it was. After returning home from work one late afternoon, someone knocked at our door. I opened the door and a thin, business-like man in a gray suit was standing there. He identified himself as a representative of the CIA; he only identified himself using the name "Alexander" and asked to talk to me. He proceeded to tell me that the information he was giving me was considered classified and I could be imprisoned if I communicated our conversation to anyone. He said to me: "A group of Cubans are organizing a brigade to invade Cuba and remove Castro and communism from the island. The brigade will consist of approximately 1,400 men, and will be trained by the CIA in an as yet undetermined Central American country." "Are you interested?" he asked. After his presentation, I felt a hollow feeling in my guts, the same sensation I felt when, as a reluctant revolutionary, I had gone off to the Escambray Mountains in search for my brother. After thinking about what he said for a few moments, I finally said that I could not make such an important decision on the spot. I wanted to think about it. He then gave me a secured telephone number and told me to get in touch with him as soon as I had come to a decision. I knew he was legitimate because of several things that he communicated to me that coincided with certain facts regarding the current situation in Cuba to which I was privy. I also knew that there was nothing he could have said to me that would have made me join. I had a premonition that this plan was destined for disaster. "Alexander" did mention the names of several of my closest friends who had been with me during the revolution and who were already in training camps in Central America and had recommended me. This was very thoughtful of them, but I made up my mind not to join this operation. I could not leave my wife all alone.

Several months later, the disaster finally occurred. On April 17, 1961, the Brigade landed at the Bay of Pigs, just south of the Mountains, in the worst possible place. I had gone swimming at Playa Larga and Playa Giron and knew exactly where the landing had taken place. The location is just south of my hometown of Colón and south of Jaguey Grande, a swampy area, with extremely difficult terrain. I wondered how the CIA's planning could have selected such a horrible target to land troops for a major military operation.

I was not surprised to learn that most of the ships were sunk and that Fidel was able to move his soldiers into the area quickly. Most of Fidel's military equipment, tanks, armored vehicles, troop trucks, passed through my hometown and some came from the city of Cienfuegos, not too far east of the landing site. The mountains are east of Cienfuegos and south of the city of Santa Clara. The explanation for choosing the area of the Bay of Pigs was due to its close proximity to the Escambray Mountains and, in case of failure, the mountains could offer a hiding place for those involved in the landing. This explanation for the selection of the Bay of Pigs was incomprehensible to me. The rugged coastline and swampy area was impassable at times. I had gone quail hunting in this area and knew it very well. I also remember the ferocity of the mosquito bites. Also, the Zapata swamp was east of the Bay of Pigs with its abundance of alligators and crocodiles, the only place in Cuba where they exist.

In spite of the optimistic news broadcast by Radio Swam that I was monitoring on my shortwave radio, I knew the Bay of Pigs operation would lead to failure from the very beginning. I learned that most of the invaders were killed. Several of my friends were among them, and the rest, were captured by Castro's soldiers.

In Washington, D.C., President John F. Kennedy had decided not to give air support to save the defeated rebel troops. At that time, I did not blame Kennedy for his action. I felt

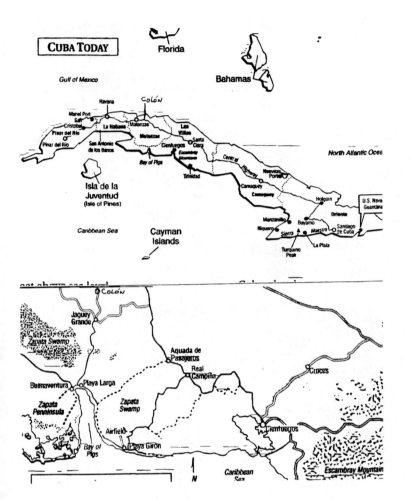

CUBA TODAY

Florida

Gulf of Mexico

Bahamas

COLÓN

Havana
Mariel Port
Baff
Cristobal
Pinar del Rio
Pinar del Rio
La Habana
San Antonio
de los Banos
Matanzas
Matanzas
Las
Villas
Santa
Clara
Cienfuegos
Escambray
Mountains
Bay of Pigs
Trinidad
Central
Highway
Nuevitas
Port
Camaguey
Camagey
North Atlantic Ocean

Isla de la
Juventud
(Isle of Pines)

Caribbean Sea

Cayman
Islands

Holguin

U.S. Naval
Guantána

Manzanillo
Niquero
Sierra
Turquino
Peak
La Plata
Bayamo
Maestra
Santiago
de Cuba
Oriente

eet above sea level

Cuba, showing

COLÓN

Jaguey
Grande

Zapata Swamp

Buenaventura
Playa Larga
Zapata
Penninsula

Aquada de
Pasajeros
Real
Campina

Croces

Zapata
Swamp

Cienfuegos

Airfield
Bay of
Pigs
Playa Girón

N

Caribbean
Sea

Escambray Mountain

that the CIA had concocted the assault plan, and that Kennedy had not had enough time to analyze the plan carefully. I felt a deep sadness for my friends who had died for nothing and hoped that those who were captured would at least come out of this military debacle with their lives. A few months later, the imprisoned rebels were released when the United States government exchanged them for agricultural equipment such as tractors, trucks, and other supplies.

A very important event occurred during the last hours of the invasion, the participation of Thomas "Pete" Ray and Leo Barker, pilot and flight engineer. They were members of the Alabama Air National Guard in Birmingham. They and their aging B-26 headed for Nicaragua and in a desperate effort to help the invasion they attacked Playa Giron and were shot down. They survived the crash landing but were murdered by Castro's soldiers. This event remained in total secret by the CIA. They did not want to recognize that American citizens were at all involved in the invasion. Only recently when materials about the Bay of Pigs invasion were declassified did the truth came out.

This happened too late for the grieving families of these heroes who gave their lives to save their friends trapped in Cuba. Someday soon, in a free Cuba, they will be honored.

On December 2, 1961, Fidel Castro, on a simultaneous radio and television broadcast, declared himself a Marxist-Leninist, a communist in our language. Now there were no more masquerades; Fidel finally had confessed to the world his plan of turning Cuba into a communist country. This was the end of Fidel Castro's hypocrisy, all the lies and cover up from the beginning of the revolution finally ended on this day. Now everybody knew the truth of the betrayal that I had understood earlier than anyone, and the main reason why I had to escape from Cuba or lose my life. I cannot help associating this situation to Adolph Hitler's betrayal of the trust of the German people, even before World War II. After Fidel's announcement, many of my friends who were working for him started to leave Cuba and sought refuge in the United States. They told me that they could not believe until that moment that Fidel was a communist. This happened, in spite of all the evidence around them.

I was never able to justify the fact that Cuba was a communist country. My wife and I donated a portion of our savings, as much as we possibly could afford in those early days, to assist those exiles that had now begun to leave Cuba. We helped those friends who had previously studied in the United States, to obtain employment; we also guaranteed some loans and used our newly acquired Sears Roebuck credit card to help some severely needy exiles to purchase their basic necessities.

While all of this was going on, my wife and I earned our Masters degrees and continued with our teaching jobs. I continued to teach Math and also the new field of Computer Science. When we had an opportunity we visited Miami for a little vacation, and we were able to keep in touch with our friends and learn more about what was going on in Cuba. I learned that many of my closest friends were still in Cuban jails and that things were very difficult for them. They suffered from lack of medical assistance, and the words "human rights" meant nothing to the jailers. I also met with their wives and sweethearts who anxiously waited for news coming out of Cuba as to their conditions and possible release.

The only good news that we received during 1960-1961 was about "Operation Peter Pan." This was about a courageous group of Cuban citizens together with members of the Catholic Church who were able to obtain falsified documents and visas under the nose of the communist authorities. This was a great risk to them but it was worth it because approximately 14,000 children managed to escape to the United States as a safe haven to them.

The new year of 1962 arrived, and I realized that it had already been over two years since my wife and I had left Cuba. My expectations to return home looked more impossible than ever, and relations between the United States and Cuba were going from bad to worse.

The summer of 1962 brought news from Cuba. Through my friends in the underground, we learned that something very big was going to happen, to be alert, and, particularly, to read the foreign press. The French and Canadian papers that I read at the University library spoke a great deal about the close relationship between Nikita Khrushchev and Fidel Castro and of the heavy imports of Russian goods and materiel into Cuba. I was hoping that there might be another attack by Cuban exiles, and perhaps at this time it would be better organized than the ill-planned Bay of Pigs invasion.

It did not take too long for me to learn what the big event was. In August of 1962, during our summer vacation in Miami, I was told by recently exiled friends that the Soviet Union had brought to Cuba a large number of troops, perhaps as many as 40,000 elite Soviet soldiers, and that very heavy equipment was being moved at night through the port of Havana, perhaps jet planes and heavy bombers. But soon we received enough information to learn that the Soviet Union was delivering rockets with nuclear warheads to Castro. We also learned that some of our friends had lost their lives retrieving this valuable information.

I was led to believe that current information about what was happening in Cuba was being passed to the CIA on a regular basis. Many months passed and absolutely no information was being published in any American newspapers. A group of exiles and I went to Washington, D.C., met with politicians from North Carolina, and presented this information about the nuclear warheads, missiles, and launch sites to them. They could not believe that Castro could be so stupid as to do such a thing. I was very nervous about what I knew. I had to ask for a short leave of absence from my teaching position to spend my time communicating with the Cubans in Miami. They had received additional evidence of crimes against human rights that were being perpetrated in Cuba. Geiger counters placed in strategic locations where the nuclear weapons were being delivered indicated nuclear material, and yet there was no news on radio, television, or the press about this new and extremely dangerous situation.

At last, information concerning the detection of Soviet surface-to-surface medium range ballistic missiles was obtained by a U2 plane flown by Air Force Major Rudolf Anderson Jr. Sadly, a few days later his plane was shot down while on a reconnaissance mission over Cuba and Major Anderson was killed. Another hero and another American victim of Fidel Castro. Together with the two American heroes of the Bay of Pigs, all three will be honored when Cuba is free again.

I was at my wits' end when finally, on October 22, 1962, in a nationwide television broadcast, President Kennedy explained that the Soviet Union had placed nuclear missile launch sites in Cuba. He called on Nikita Khrushchev of the Soviet Union to either dismantle all missile launch sites and to remove all military equipment or the United States would launch a nuclear ballistic missile attack on Cuba.

I was very excited because of the heavy movement of troops from bases in North Carolina and naval movements in Norfolk, Virginia, where I had many friends. Everybody I knew was very excited; some colleagues from the University came to talk to us with the conviction that this time we would be able to return home. It was our belief that the United States would never allow communism to continue on an island only 90 miles from its shores. Despite this fact, and knowing the true spirit of Fidel Castro and his intense hate for the United States, I felt these were truly extremely dangerous times. I feared the worst; a nuclear war between the Soviet Union and the United States which would mean instant death for my family and all of the citizens of Cuba. Many of my students at the university were members of the 82nd Airborne Division and had been called to active duty. I knew from their insinuations that there was a major operation in the works and that they truly believed that their units would be in Havana the next morning.

Finally, after days of agonizing expectations it happened; the Soviet Union agreed to remove their missiles under the condition that the United States would never invade Cuba.

When I first heard of this condition mandated by the Soviet Union, I did not realize the impact that this would have on my life and on the lives of the exiled Cubans in

President John F Kennedy signing the
Order for the Cuban blockade

October 23 1962

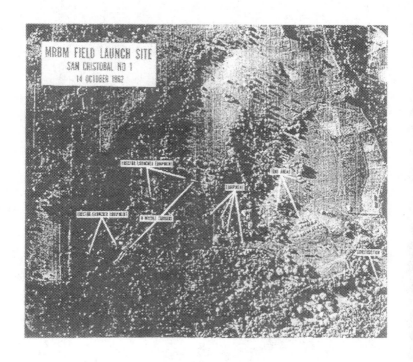

National Security Archives Document

October 14, 1962

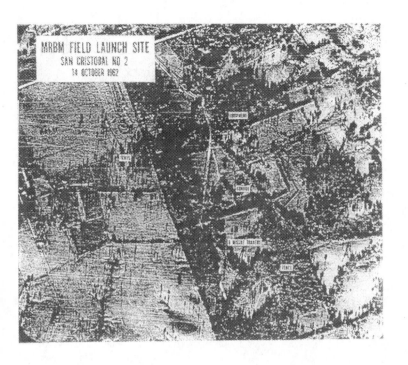

National Security Archives Document

October 14, 1962

National Security Archives Document
October 23, 1962

National Security Archives Document

October 27, 1962

the United States. As time went by and I received more information, I felt the same way I felt when I realized that Fidel Castro was going to turn Cuba into a communist country, that is, I felt betrayed. How could President Kennedy agree to allow Castro and his murderers to remain in control in Cuba? I also understood that no Latin American country would dare to allow the exile community to launch any invasion or attack from their shores. Most of these countries owed their survival to the American aid they were receiving. From Mexico with its anti-American feelings down to the American colony of Panama and Central America, nobody would dare go against the position taken by President John Kennedy.

It was then that I realized that my wife, my parents, my friends, other exiles, and I had lost our country for good. Our dreams of returning home one day would not be fulfilled. At this time I told my wife, "I don't think we will be going home in the near future. Let's work, earn our Ph.D. degrees, and move to Connecticut." There I had been offered a full professor position and we could purchase a spacious, comfortable home; make enough money so that we will be financially secure; start planning a family; and, in general, live as well as our combined talents would allow us.

Chapter Nine: The Interim: From Then to Now

While we were trying to normalize our lives in the United States, Cuba established close relations with the Soviet Union and served as a Soviet surrogate in Africa and several countries in Latin America. "Surrogate" means that since Castro could not pay in cash for the billions of dollars that the Soviet Union was sending to Cuba, Castro would send in return agents such as: Che, Ochoa, and Dr. Mell among others and weapons to those countries. Then, in 1975, Cuba launched a major intervention in Africa. Cuban blood was shed there, first in Algeria, and later in the Congo (now Zaire) Thousands of Cuba's best sons offered their lives for the independence and sovereignty of the African countries. After the Congo they fought in Angola, Guinea Bissau, Cape Verdi,

Che Guevara on the left

Dr.Oscar Fernadez Mell on the right

The Congo (Zaire)
1965

Mozambique, and Namibia. The bodies of the mostly black Cuban soldiers were flown back to Cuba. They arrived at night in order to hide this event from the citizens of Cuba. When the bodies became too many, then they were buried in Africa. We learned all this from the relatives of those killed who had gotten out and were in exile in South Florida. Castro also deployed troops in Ethiopia, and North Africa, and allowed more Soviet forces in Cuba. The Soviets established a listening station at Lourdes, south of Havana, to monitor the communications from the United States. My only thought about all this was that the Soviet Union with their food shortage and lack of consumer goods could not prop up Cuba and their own empire forever. Still, I could not understand how the United States tolerated all these events.

Then, in April 1980, news came out of Cuba that an estimated 10,000 Cubans had stormed the Peruvian Embassy in Havana seeking political asylum. Due to the embarrassment caused by this action, the Cuban government allowed 125,000 Cubans to illegally depart for the United States from the port of Mariel, the so-called: "Mariel boatlift." Castro took advantage of this exodus and sent a good number of criminals and mentally ill persons with this boatlift. Once again, though I felt happy for those leaving the Cuban hell, I quickly recognized that this boatlift was nothing but an escape valve that would extend the life of communism in Cuba. The president responsible was Jimmy Carter. For the second time another American president was outsmarted by Fidel Castro. Since then, we have witnessed one migration after another. In August 1994, the Cuban government allowed some 30,000 Cubans to set sail for the United States in unsafe boats and rafts, which resulted in a number of deaths at sea. The 90 mile stretch between Cuba and Key West is a shark infested sea and many families whose rel

never heard back from t

On July 13, 1994, v

Cuba, the tugboat "13 de Marzo" was attacked by agents of the Cuban government. They repeatedly rammed the tug, used high-pressure water hoses on the victims, and sank the ship seven miles off the coast of Havana. At least 41 men, women and children died in the "13 de Marzo" Massacre. Their bodies are still inside the tug. Unfortunately, many Americans do not know about this serious crime.

On February 24, 1996, the Cuban military under direct orders of Fidel Castro, shot down two U.S. civil aircraft in international space, killing three U.S. citizens and one U.S. resident. The American Air Force did nothing to prevent this tragedy from occurring. Once before, during the Bay of Pigs invasion, the United States failed to assist the invading Brigade by not helping to destroy Castro's Air Force. The crimes of Fidel Castro's regime are well documented and yet here we are, still in the U.S. awaiting the miracle of the liberation of Cuba from communism after 42 years of suffering.

What happened to my friends, relatives, and associates?

In 1966, Rolando Cubela was sentenced to twenty-five years in jail for plotting to kill Fidel Castro. He seemed to have been working for the CIA, but Castro later pardoned him. Why? I guess only Castro knows; perhaps he was really a double agent.

How much pain Rolando Cubela would have saved Cuba had he succeeded! Regardless, he is now a physician living in Spain. Che died in Bolivia in 1967, executed by a Bolivian military force. I would have shed a tear had he been killed during the battle for Santa Clara, but not now, considering all the crimes he committed after the revolution ended. He finally behaved as the true communist that he was. I only regret that he did not live long enough to see the horrible damage that communism had brought to Cuba.

President Urrutia died in 1981, and his replacement, Eduardo Dorticos, committed suicide in 1983. Some people said that he was disappointed with the Castros' betrayal of the revolution.

My friends, Mongo and Pepe Garcia, were released from prison after twenty-five years. They arrived in Miami and married their teenage sweethearts who had been waiting all those years and remained true to them. They both shortly produced a set of twins each. This was wonderful news, making up for the lost time. They never surrendered, even though I had begged them through underground mail to sign the paper that could have released them. The paper stated that they would not do anything against the revolution. At a time when the American presidents were kissing Soviet Premiers and détente was in style, I thought they should sign the documents and travel to the United States. When we finally met in Miami, I told them that I would have signed such a document in order to get out of Cuba. They replied that I would not have signed it because if I had been in prison as long as they had I would never have considered giving Fidel the satisfaction. Anyway, I was very proud of them.

In 1965 the situation in Cuba had become so intolerable, that, my sister had to leave my family and come to Connecticut with her husband and their 7-year old daughter.

My father and mother died in Cuba, never having the opportunity to return to Spain; their love for Cuba was too great to abandon it. They both died very young and totally heartbroken. A few years later my brother Pepe also died from a simple gall bladder operation. His death was brought about by the poor Russian medicine and the terrible medical care in Cuba. I was not able to go to

Cuba for their funerals for obvious reasons. If I had gone to their funerals I would have been tortured and imprisoned, at best, shot, at worst.

I will always regret that I could not share my life with them since I left them that summer of 1959. They were never able to meet my two lovely daughters or see how successful their son had become, a university professor, a consultant to major corporations, a respected computer scientist, and now, a writer.

My dear friend Dr. Oscar Fernandez Mell remained in Cuba and he is now one of the "empayamados" or "in pajamas," which means that he is under house arrest. He will remain under house arrest for the rest of his life, or until Fidel Castro dies. This is shocking for a man who was so close to Che and who was involved in the African expedition, one of the last survivors of the Cuban saga.

As for my dear friend Rolando Gonzalez, "Palillo," who helped me when I wanted to go after my brother in the Escambray, I arranged for him to go to Canada. Because he had made the mistake of joining the Communist Party in order to advance in his position, not for political conviction, he could not migrate to the United States. He finally ended up in Sydney, Australia, where he is presently a successful electrical engineer.

Every occasion we have, my family likes to travel to Miami Beach to visit relatives and to visit cemeteries in Miami and South Florida where some of our relatives and friends are buried. It never ceases to amaze us that these cemeteries are filled with the graves of hundred of thousands of Cubans. Most of them were country people, laborers, truck drivers, and blue-collar workers, as well as teachers, doctors, and lawyers. All of them are buried there because they did not want to live in a communist country. As the years go by, the rest of the more than two million exiles will join them. The Cuban exiles are the victims of the inability of the leaders of the United States to stop the communist government of one man: Fidel Castro. The Cubans who died in the United States will not have a Babi Yar Monument or an Arlington Cemetery to honor them. Cuban-Americans do not have a good public relations office, and Hollywood will never present the history of Cuba in its true image. They are more interested in portraying Castro and Che as mythical heroes, not the traitors and butchers they are.

After more than forty-two years in the United States, I still burn with the desire to return to my homeland of Cuba. I am grateful to the United States of America where my daughters were born free of spirit and soul. I would love to be able to visit the graves of my family in my hometown of Colón and perhaps someday be buried next to them. In my last will and testament I have requested to have the Cuban flag that my mother made on her sewing machine and a bouquet of white roses placed with me in my coffin.

As José Marti, Cuba's greatest patriot, stated in one of his poems, "Yo quiero cuando me muera, sin patria pero sin amo, tener en mi tumba un ramo de flores y una bandera." "When I die, without a country but without a master, I wish to have in my grave a bouquet of flowers and a flag."

It is my hope that this memoir will help others in the world's community to understand the tragedy of the Cuban people. The world needs to acknowledge the suffering of the Cuban people. Many Cubans were forced to abandon their homes, their families, and their livelihoods. Cuban nationals who rejected Castro's communistic rule and fled Cuba, as well as all of the Cubans who stayed in Cuba, willingly or unwillingly, have been pawns of the international intrigues between two superpowers: the United States of America and the Union of Soviet Socialist Republics.

Now, the Cubans from all over the world as well as those in the island of Cuba are patiently awaiting Castro's death. We believe that it is the destiny of Cuba to be a free nation again. Also there is no one with Castro's charisma to take his place. What really upsets most Cubans is that the Soviet Union does not exist anymore, so the United States does not have to protect Fidel Castro anymore. Remember that the promise that John Kennedy made to them had created the fact that the Cubans had to come here in exile. The damage done by the Cuban communist government in countries such as Nicaragua, El Salvador, Guatemala and Colombia as well as its support to any anti-American group around the world has been enormous. And yet, no president of the United States since Kennedy has dared to act. The Americans have their Viet Nan defeat mentality, and the Cubans in exile have the

Bay of Pigs and the Missile Crisis as their defeat mentality.

After all these years, the American press continues to ignore events in Cuba, not to write about abuses of human rights, the lack of freedom, the scarcity of food and medicine, and on and on. They seem to be more concerned with establishing relations and removing the embargo in order for the American government to give Castro credit to purchase goods in the United States. The morality of those who want to enrich themselves collides with the desire of the Cubans to have a free government on the island, a government that will respect human rights and the rights of the individual. We would like to return to our motherland but only when it is free, unlike those tourists that go to Cuba for rest and recreation while seemingly oblivious to the poverty and misery being suffered by the masses.

The embargo on the Soviet Union by the United States worked because our allies in Europe and Canada backed us up, but that is not the case with Cuba. Anybody in the world can go to Cuba, except the American people and those Cubans of high morality. In 42 years no past or present president of the United States has taken a true position to liberate Cuba and end this tragedy. Otherwise, I would already be in Cuba, no longer a reluctant revolutionary but just another Cuban going back home.

THE END

AUTHOR'S NOTE

I would like to suggest that after reading this book you would go to the Internet and search for the topics covered in this narration of my personal experience. This would add validity and support to my many points of view. Freedom is too important an issue to treat it lightly.

ISBN 1553956060-0

9 781553 956068